Insights 2
Reflection and Introspection

By Dr. Jaya Sonkar, MD MPH

HOBBIES AND HAPPINESS CREATIONS
Texas, USA

Published by Hobbies and Happiness Creations 2024
Copyright Dr. Jaya Sonkar MD MPH 2024

Dedication

This book is dedicated to my daughter, Ms. Riya Agarwal; my beloved parents, Mr. Ram Baboo Sonkar and Mrs. Ranjana Sonkar; and my cherished family and friends. I extend my heartfelt gratitude to my teachers, patients, colleagues, business partners, vendors, and everyone I have ever met. Each meeting and every interaction has contributed to my learning journey, and the process continues.

Index

Contents

Poems

The Mind Vibes

Has it ever happened that you suddenly look at someone and realize that person was looking at you? Or if you have been looking at someone, does that person suddenly turn to you?

Just the other day, I took my daughter and her friend to a show. We were all engrossed in watching it when suddenly I turned around and found two eyes looking at me.

That was strange. It didn't bother me that those eyes were watching me; what bothered me was that they seemed to have the power to make me turn back and look at them.

What was that? This happens often. Most of us may have experienced it at some point.

Just like light and sound waves, there is probably something like mind waves that travel. There has to be something that connects our minds. The people we are close to probably share a special connection.

We all know the principles of resonance. How is it possible for a distant window to vibrate due to music far away?

How is it possible for a star that is billions of light-years away to be visible to us?

We know magnetism exists. There is something that attracts and something that repels. There is an essence in everything and every living being that attracts or repels.

If nature made us, it must have utilized all its phenomena to create a wonderful life.

We can prove light energy because we can see it; we can prove sound energy because we can hear it; we can prove resonance because it is perceivable in the form of vibrations when the frequencies match; and we can prove magnetism because we can feel the force on an object when it is pushed or pulled.

It is hard to explain, prove, or quantify the mind's vibes, but they are there, and we all know that to a certain extent. It is a phenomenon that connects humans with the rest of the universe, and we are all part of the same universe.

This also suggests that no one is superior or inferior. There can be some trivial physical and mental traits that may deceive us into believing one person is greater than another. Everyone strives hard to prove their worth, but the truth is that everyone is a product of the same universe and made of the same elements. I wouldn't limit this to five elements, as we don't know if there are sixth, seventh, eighth, or more elements yet to be discovered.

Something in the vacuum of space is filled with strange matter—matter that connects us all.

For the same reasons, we often intuit the inner intentions of others we interact with. If we activate our perception channels, we can receive an enormous amount of information and awareness that is available to us at all times.

Words are often ornamental; more than half of communication occurs without them. Perhaps our minds are inherently trained to interpret the meanings of subtle gestures, expressions, and even silence.

We can activate our signaling system to open the channels that relay our inner selves to the universe and open ourselves to an amazing world that has been waiting for our exploration.

Spiritual energy does not embody sadness, happiness, pain, or pleasure; it simply exists quietly.

We should strive to align with similar energies and let them flow in the direction they want to go to maintain peace and harmony within ourselves.

Let's follow the flow of nature, open our mind's eyes, and feel the mind's vibes.

Photograph by: Dr. Jaya Sonkar MD MPH

Life ... with or without the weight!

Weight change can alter the way we look at life!

Can this teach us about the concept of the life within us? Let's take a look!

Have you or anyone you know ever experienced weight loss?
What is weight made up of?

Food, water, air?

What is food made of?

Earth, water, air, sunlight, and fire generate minerals, vitamins, carbohydrates, proteins, and fats, which in turn result in the formation of different parts of the body.

Now, let's say Person X wants to reduce their weight. After losing 1 lb, Person X is still Person X. After losing 10 lbs, Person X is still Person X. After losing 20 lbs, Person X is still Person X. After losing 100 lbs, Person X is still Person X.

After losing all the weight, is Person X still Person X, minus the body?

Losing and gaining weight is just the loss or accumulation of substances from the Earth and space. However, is there something inside us that accumulates weight and sheds it off?

Or is it like a computer?

A computer can see with its camera, think, reflect, and produce results on the screen; it can hear with a mic and speak with its speakers.

A computer is made from elements of the Earth, and when the parts are disassembled, it's not a computer anymore. However, a computer doesn't have life within it.

Weight loss or weight gain sheds light on the enigma of life in its own unique way.
What is this life within us made of?

Or is it just there?

Does it have a tendency or nature, just like every non-living thing?
Whatever it is, it has the same potential as any other life within any other body.

And this life is what connects us all!

Are we all one?

Photograph by: Dr. Jaya Sonkar MD MPH

Could consciousness seep into robots?

While exploring the possibility of traces of water and life on other celestial bodies, my imagination ignites, prompting the question: how do we know that other life forms thrive solely on water? Who knows—perhaps they could be composed of metal, existing on liquid natural gas.

I find myself wondering: in places that are not conducive to earthly life forms, are they truly incapable of supporting any type of life?

A deeper layer of thought begins to penetrate my mind.

If the heart ceases to beat, pacemakers or medications—essentially chemicals—can provide support. If a limb is amputated, prosthetics can assist; if there is lung or kidney failure, transplants offer a solution; if blood is depleted, transfusions come to the rescue... We can be constructed of plastic, metal, and wires, yet still feel undeniably alive.

Could robots ever attain consciousness? Is it possible for life to inhabit them?

Photograph by: Dr. Jaya Sonkar MD MPH

What's the goal?

Commonly, we try to anchor ourselves to some goal at every phase of life. When we are born, our primary goal is survival. As children, our goal shifts to studying, achieving good grades, and eventually gaining admission to a prestigious academic institution. Once we reach that stage, we seek a good job. With financial stability, we desire to settle down. When we find the life partner of our dreams and have children, our focus turns to raising them and, ultimately, nurturing our grandchildren.

The continuity of our species is deeply embedded in our DNA. This instinct is crucial; without it, our species would dwindle away.

However, once we have a surplus of everything, what then becomes our next goal?

There must be something more to life than mere survival, the   continuation of our species, and the accumulation of material resources to ensure the comfort of future generations.

What more is there? If we lack a goal, if we don't have an aim that could stimulate our dopamine receptors, then what are we truly longing for?

Is there a deeply buried vision within us that yearns to emerge and live fully?

Once we achieve everything and feel satisfied, what do we then crave?

A few days ago, I met a beautiful elderly patient, Mrs. Jones, in her late 80s.

She said, "I am very satisfied with my life. I had a wonderful partner, caring children, and everything has been truly good. Now, I am ready to go."

She added, "I just want to stay comfortable for as long as I am here." Then she asked with a smile, "Doctor, can you give me a shot in my knee? It's hurting and affecting my mobility."

I smiled and examined her. She was stable enough

to receive a knee injection for her osteoarthritis. It provided her some relief, and she rewarded me with a warm smile and a hug.

That hug was truly wonderful. It transmitted her satisfaction to me, and I felt genuinely happy to see her content.

I left the facility, but Mrs. Jones lingered in my thoughts.

Is the ultimate goal of Mrs. Jones' life simply to raise children, lead a fulfilling life, and ultimately seek a comfortable passing?

Isn't that often our goal as well? It's a good goal to have, and indeed, my patient seemed very happy with it.

What if we don't have a goal? What do we live for then? Or do we find ourselves feeling done with life?

What goal does our universe have?

It just exists. So many celestial bodies revolve aimlessly around one another—thoughtlessly, mindlessly, and fearlessly. Fearlessly, because there's always the risk of colliding with another celestial body, which could lead to complete destruction.

What is their goal? Is it merely to exist?

What is the goal of the ocean, which generates waves every second? It simply exists and responds to the forces acting upon it.

When we achieve everything we desire, what else can we do to feel that same pleasure? Brands emerge from this need to feel happiness by showcasing our achievements, creating additional goals for others to aspire to, which display their accomplishments thus far.

Getting trapped in this mindset feels like being ensnared in a vicious circle—one goal after another, in hopes of reaching an ultimate aim.

However, attaining that so-called ultimate goal often reveals that it wasn't truly ultimate after all. As long as we live, we keep wanting more—more material possessions or selfless joy from wishing for our loved ones' happiness. Eventually, when we tire of this relentless pursuit, we may make death our ultimate goal.

What guarantees that death is the ultimate goal?

Could there be more to it?

It's a very intriguing thought!

For now, perhaps simply feeling accomplished without having a defined goal is itself a worthy goal.

This doesn't mean we should stop doing what we're doing. It simply suggests that we keep moving forward without fixating on completion.

Perhaps achieving without a specific goal is the goal—a goal to exist happily and engage in what we truly care about.

Maybe that's why it's said, "Karma Kar, phal ki chinta mat Kar."

We should give our best in everything we do, enjoying the process and the company we keep at each step. This seems to be the pathway toward understanding this enigma…

What's the goal?
What's the purpose?

Photograph by: Dr. Jaya Sonkar MD MPH

Acceptance

Acceptance of the present and determination to improve the future are key to a happy and successful life.

What has already happened cannot be changed unless we build a time machine to go back to the past.

What is happening in the present is also unavoidable; it is happening already.

What will happen in the future is within our control. While it is very common for occurrences to follow a pattern, allowing us to predict the next moment, the possibilities for unexpected occurrences are enormous.

Furthermore, our capacity to shape the future is vast.

It depends on our thoughts on how we mold our actions to produce the desired results.

Let's take an example: Let's say the beautiful, one-of-a-kind, rare, irreplaceable, and expensive crystal glass that was in our hands has broken. Can we bring the glass back now?

We can spend time feeling sad about it, but that won't bring the glass back.

Can it? The sooner we realize that it's broken and clean up the pieces, the sooner we will have a clearer space, reducing the chances of injury from those shards.

The beauty of the glass will remain in our memory as a pleasant thought, and we can find happiness as soon as we accept that it's gone, that it can't come back, and that we can't change the past.

What we can change is the future. We can put precautions in place to prevent similar incidents from happening again.

However, lingering on the loss is merely a function of our memory. The more we learn to control and navigate it to our advantage, the sooner we will discover how to be happy.

Nothing is permanent except change itself; we know that things will change.

Everything has a limited lifespan. Even the sun and stars have a lifespan.

The example above pertains to a mundane object. However, the concept applies to any living or non-living thing. It applies to humans too.

Any previous experience, good or bad, can only hurt us if we allow it to.

Once we accept the present and move on, we can start on the path to happiness.

After all, happiness is a state of mind, and the mind can be controlled.

Isn't that true?

Photograph by: Dr. Jaya Sonkar MD MPH

Let's drive!

Let's drive to our chosen destiny!

We all know that we can behave as social animals, as we have the capacity to follow Yama and Niyamas.

We can adhere to the norms of society and practice self-discipline.

If we excel in this and gain complete control, then we can responsibly drive our human bodies to achieve our desired destinations.

Let's take a simple example.

Do you ever hit the snooze button? Let's imagine a beautiful morning.

We want to snooze for 5 minutes, then another 3 minutes, and then another 2 minutes until we finally wake up.

At the end of the last snooze, something in our thoughts prompts our body into action, and we wake up to start our day.

Now, let's consider another simple example.

We have to prepare for an upcoming test or finish an assignment.
However, there's a nice movie we want to watch, or we might check our social media, go out, or do anything else of our choice.

We think about how we need to prepare for the upcoming test or complete the assignment.

We think about it once, then again, and eventually, we do it.

What was in that final thought before we eventually acted that the previous thoughts didn't contain?

What made it turn into action?

It was a conscious control that overpowered our

reflexes and the natural instincts of every cell, allowing us to direct them toward the outcome we desired.

Let's say we have the most expensive car in the world, which can offer a lot of comfort, speed, and joy. But if we don't know how to drive it, we might drive haphazardly and end up in an accident.

There has to be something within us that we came here to achieve, which would give us that sense of fulfillment—the most gratifying experience leading to Nirvana.

We probably select where we want to go, where we want to be raised, and what kind of skill set we wish to acquire.

Let's say a pilot wants to fly; the pilot will choose an airplane as the vehicle, not a car.

If a car racer wants to race, they will find the best car.

If a cab driver wants a vehicle to bring commuters to their destination, the cab driver will seek the most efficient and safe option.

If a motorcyclist wants to feel the thrill of balance and speed, they will choose a motorcycle.

If a biker needs speed, exercise, and the endorphins released from physical effort, they will opt for a bicycle.

If a horse rider desires the thrill of controlling a wild horse and taking it for a ride to a destination, the horse rider will choose a horse as their carriage.

The crux of the matter is that whatever we have is enough for us to fulfill our desires.
If we have a desire, we also possess the capability to fulfill it.
What is needed is aim, effort, determination, self-control, and mastery over our mind and body to achieve it.

Only then can we drive safely and reach where we want to go when we want to go.

We always want to do something. Let's ensure we follow what we truly desire and always find a way to achieve it.

Are we ready to drive?

Photograph by: Dr. Jaya Sonkar MD MPH

Who Benefits?

Who Benefits?

If one is good to the other, who benefits the most?

1. One who is good
2. One who gets the goodness
3. Both benefit equally
4. None
5. Unsure

If one does good deeds but expects nothing in return, who benefits the most?

1. One who does the good deed but doesn't expect.
2. One who receives the good deed
3. Both benefit equally
4. None

5. Unsure

If one focuses on the good actions but doesn't worry about the results, who benefits the most?

1. One who does the action
2. One who watches the action being done
3. One who is receiving the action
4. None
5. Unsure

Would you say that our ancestors, who promoted the following principles, wanted us to be altruistic and renounce the world?

'Be a good samaritan'
'Neki Kar Dariya Mein Daal' (Do good and don't expect anything in return)
'Karm Kar Phal Ki Chinta Na Kar' (Focus on actions and not the results)

Who Benefits from all of the above?

It's the one who does these.

How?

When we do good to others in our capacity without

harming ourselves or our loved ones, it generates a feeling of happiness, peace, and calm.

Whose body would benefit from feeling calm and happy?
The Doer's.

Whose stress level will be low?
The Doer's

Who's BP, Blood Sugar, heart health, and mental health will be at its best?
The Doer's

If one focuses on the aim and doesn't get distracted or worried about the possible outcomes, who would have better chances of success?

The Doer's
No one else but the Doer's focus will not dwindle and chances of success will be at their maximum.

And if despite all efforts, the outcomes are different then it just needs to be tried harder.

Our ancestors were not thinking about anyone else's well-being but the Doer's well-being.

Let's say if you get a bad rear end because of someone who wasn't paying attention to their driving and forgot to apply brakes at a red light and hit you from behind, if one gets upset with that person and feels angry, who is at a bigger loss?

One loss has happened, and the car has been damaged.

Hopefully, the health is fine. Let's assume the health is fine and no bodily injuries.

Now, drilling that person down would not help with anything. Should one ask for one's rightful remediation?

Absolutely yes.

However, the peaceful space in our minds should stay peaceful despite everything going around.

No one should have the power to enter our minds and bother it.

Let's say, now the car goes to the collision center.

The collision center and the insurance team up to work on a cheap repair and the collision center fraudulently bills the insurance for new parts but applies old sourced parts and gives the car to one in a not-good condition.

How should one react?

Well, certainly fight for the rightful repair and ask for a genuine fix.
However, should one feel angry or ill will for them?

No, because it would not benefit one. The damage has already been done. The focus should always be on fixing the issue but again no one should be able to enter one's happy space in the mind and corrupt it because that will be a bigger loss.

Let's say one writes a book with passion and someone tries to blackmail one into paying for reviews and gives one a bad review for not accepting their offer.

Would one benefit from being angry?

Clearly, one should not give in to such requests.

However, bringing a feeling of kindness towards someone who is interested in reading and may be going through some financial hardship or perhaps is trying to make a living somehow by using these sources, would benefit the author more than being upset.

While wrong deeds should not be encouraged, they should also not be allowed to enter the peaceful space in one's mind and affect one's happiness.

If one does a good deed but keeps expecting something in return, one only creates a path of misery and sadness if the reciprocation doesn't happen.

One should do only that much that one could do and let go of the expectation of reciprocation.

That way, if the reciprocation doesn't happen, it doesn't affect at all and if it does then one should let the other person experience the goodness within them by being a recipient and feel the gratitude towards the one who reciprocated.

A good deed with an expectation is not a good deed anymore, it becomes business. And business with no returns is an unpleasant loss.
Hence a good deed should always happen without an expectation of reciprocation.

Forgiveness, peace and calm, and focus on one's

actions without worrying, benefit those the most who follow these.

These are very selfish things because they aim at self well-being the most.

There is no point wasting even a second of precious life, thinking about something unpleasant.

Instead, being pleasant and spreading peace and harmony with a smile benefits one and all, especially the one who does these.

When our ancestors wrote these idioms and taught these principles, they wanted us to be absolutely selfish and not let anything affect the happy space in our mind so we collect the best karma on the way.

Are we ready to be selfish in a good way?

Photograph by: Dr. Jaya Sonkar MD MPH

You are You because They are They!

You are You because They are They!

Let's see this in detail.

We interact with the universe every second.

If the earth wasn't Earth, we wouldn't be living as we are

If the sun wasn't shining, we wouldn't be thriving as we are.

If the water wasn't water, life wouldn't be flowing within us the way it does.

If the air wasn't air, we wouldn't be breathing as we do.

If the farmers weren't farmers, we probably wouldn't have enough and would have to farm for ourselves.

If the cleaners weren't there, we probably wouldn't get the hygienic and beautiful surroundings and would have to work much harder to maintain that.

If the plumbers weren't there, we wouldn't get the water supply and drainage as we do.

If the electricians weren't there, we wouldn't get electricity the way we do and many of us would have been injured by electric shock.

If the entertainers weren't there, we wouldn't have been amused the way we do.

If the engineers weren't there, we wouldn't get megastructures or infrastructure or modes of communication or transport developed.

If the architects weren't there, we wouldn't have safe buildings, bridges, roads etc

If the construction workers weren't there, we wouldn't be able to see this beautifully constructed society.

If the miners were not there, we wouldn't have seen the beautiful gemstones and precious metals.

If the astronauts were not there we wouldn't have known about the universe the way we do.

If the researchers were not there, we wouldn't have known so much about so many things.

If the teachers wouldn't teach, the students wouldn't learn the way they do.

If the authors didn't write, the knowledge wouldn't be able to propagate the way it does.

If the nurses and health technicians were not there, we wouldn't get the medical care at times of need.

If the doctors were not there, we wouldn't have the health and longevity the way we do.

If the evil wasn't there, we wouldn't have appreciated the goodness the way we do.

If the goodness wasn't there, we wouldn't have experienced peace the way we do.
If the parents were not there, we wouldn't have been born.

If the children were not there, life would come to a halt.

If everyone was not doing what they do, we wouldn't be living in the world that we do.

Everyone is important.
Every work is important.
Every belief is important.
Every behavior is important.
Every action is important.
Every reaction is important.

Everything deserves respect.
Everyone deserves respect.
Everything has a meaning.
And everything makes Us, 'Us'!

Poems

Photograph by: Dr. Jaya Sonkar MD MPH

We Are United!

We are united!

We breathe the same air
We drink the same water
We all are carved out of earth
Within us is the same fire

We all are born
We all will die
We all are the part
Of the same blue sky

We all have feelings
We all have emotions
We all have the flaws
We all have the wisdom

We all have to learn
We all are in a school
We follow nature's laws
We follow nature's rules

We are all creations
Of some unknown creator
We clearly are here for something
We are in this together

It's said God is everywhere
It's probably true
God is within all of us
We are all part of God

The God who is everything
The God who is everywhere
The God who is a creator
God lives in all creations!

Let's fly to the moon!

Let's fly to the moon!

Come,
Hold my hand
I will take you to the moon

We will fly
We'll have our sky
And I will see you very soon

Join me
In this ride
It is full of high tides

I will embrace you
And encase you
And bring you safely to the sides

It will be
All fine one day
It will see a shining sun

It will see
The lush greens
Where we'll go for our run

We will run
Up and down
The beautiful meadows

We will play
We will laugh
We'll have all fun and no woes

Trust me
We will soon
Find our own sweet nest

Where
We will thrive, not just survive
We will have a great zest

Believe me,
Life is full of roller coasters
It's fun if you learn to ride

Its worth
To learn and ace it
And be your own guide

Then,
You can hold one
And guide to the moon

There will be
Mirth and laughter
Everywhere very soon

Come,
Hold my hand
I will take you to the moon

We will fly
And have our sky
And I will see you very soon!

Photograph by: Dr. Jaya Sonkar MD MPH

If This Is There, That Will Be There

Ye Hai To Woh Bhi Hoga
(Translation to English included)

Jahan gulab hai, wahan Kuch to chubhega
Jahan Suraj hai, wahan Kuch to jalega

Jahan heera hai, wahan tez dhar bhi hogi
Jahan nadi hai, wahan baadh bhi hogi

Jahan Raste Hain, wahan safar bhi hoga
Jahan bachav hai, wahan gadar bhi hoga

Jahan roshni hai, chakachaundh bhi hogi
Jahan pawan hai, wahan aandhi bhi hogi

Jahan chadhav hai, wahan utaar bhi hoga
Jahan Chandrama hai, wahan andhakar bhi hoga

Jahan Kamal hai, wahan keechad bhi hoga
Jahan achha hai, wahan bura bhi hoga

Jahan pyar hai, wahan takraar bhi hogi
Jahan Jeet hai, wahan haar bhi hogi

Yadi ek pehlu hai, to doosra bhi hoga
Yadi ek nehla hai, to dehla bhi hoga

Jahan rechak hai, wahan poorak bhi hoga
Jahan mrityu hai, wahan Jeevan bhi hoga

Poem written in Hindi
Below is the translation to English

If this is there, that will be there too!

Where there is a rose, there will also be thorns
Where there's sunlight, there will also be burns

Where there's a shining diamond, there will also be
a sharp edge
Where there's flowing river, there will also be a
flood

Where there are ways, there will also be ups and
downs

Where there is protection, there will also be a rebel-
lion

Where there will be light, there will also be blind-
ness
Where there is wind, there will also be a storm

Where there are ups, there will also be downs
Where there are full moon nights ,there will also be
darkness

Where there is a lotus, there will be mud
Where there is good, there will be bad

Where there's love, there will also be hate
Where there is a win, there will also be a loss

If there is one side of the coin, there will also be the
other
If there is a nine, there will also be a ten

When we exhale, we also inhale
Where there is a death, there is also a life.

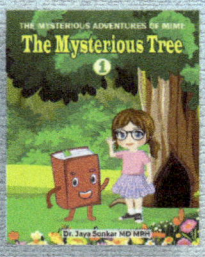

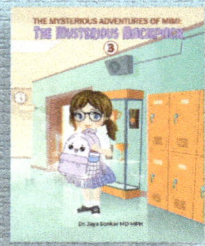
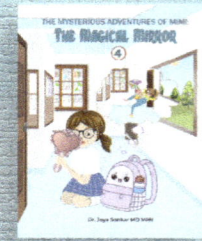

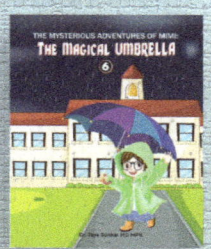

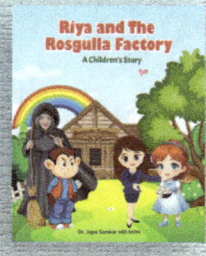

THE END

www.ingramcontent.com/pod-product-compliance
Lightning Source LLC
Chambersburg PA
CBHW061719120626
46550CB00003B/1284